Presented to:

_____

From:

_____

Date:

_____

Get Unstuck & Stay Unstuck

Because **Fear** Is **Not** the **Boss** of You

JENNIFER ALLWOOD

ZONDERVAN

ZONDERVAN

Get Unstuck & Stay Unstuck
© 2022 Jennifer Allwood

Requests for information should be addressed to:
Zondervan, *3900 Sparks Dr. SE, Grand Rapids, Michigan 49546*

ISBN 978-0-310-45520-2 (audio book)
ISBN 978-0-310-45499-1 (eBook)
ISBN 978-0-310-45564-6 (HC)

Art direction and cover design: Sabryna Lugge
Cover illustration and lettering: Jessi Raulet
Interior design: Denise Froehlich
Photography credit, page 154: Amber Deery, Amber Deery Photography

Printed in China

22 23 24 25 26 27 28 29 30 GRI 15 14 13 12 11 10 9 8 7 6 5 4 3 2 1

This book is dedicated to my mother, Connie Edwards.
Mom, you could have stayed stuck but you refused to.
Thank you for being brave with your life so
that I could be brave with mine.
I love you!!

And to my husband, Jason. My favorite human ever.
I'm so glad we didn't stay stuck. I love you more.

CONTENTS

> You are completely capable of having a
> life filled with peace and deep joy and
> expectancy. A life without stuck. A life without
> overwhelm. That is a life worth living.
>
> **Jennifer Allwood**

Are you feeling stuck?

No one ever wants to be stuck, but it happens. And when it does it can be so dang hard to get unstuck. I know because I've been there, and if you're reading this book, you're probably either feeling stuck right now or have in the past. And doesn't it stink?

Being stuck drains your peace and joy and sucks the life right out of you. It makes you feel hopeless about your current situation, like there's something wrong with you because you should be able to get out of the rut you're in, right?

It makes you look around and wonder why no one else seems

stuck on the sidelines. Your best friend, the mom you chat with at PTA meetings, and especially the woman who runs your favorite Instagram account—they all seem to be doing big things, bubbling over with excitement about their activities and jobs, and just generally living their best lives. And that makes you feel even worse about your current situation.

That's what stuck does. It pulls you into comparison traps and makes you believe the lies that "it will always be this way" and "you can never" and "if only." Slowly you start to believe that your situation, your relationship, your job—your *life*—are the only ones stuck and that it will always be this way.

Stuck people · stick people.

The thing is, being stuck doesn't just affect *you*. It impacts everything and everyone you touch, and it drains the life from the people in your world. When you're stuck it's impossible to be the best *you* that you can be. Your spouse will feel it. So will your kids. And your friends. You were never meant to stay stuck. Your family and friends need you unstuck. The world needs you free to do what you were made to do.

Stuck people stay small. When you're stuck, you don't take risks or chances, no matter how exciting they are. You miss out on so many of the things that God has planned for you because you're too stuck to claim them. And when you stay small, all the people you are meant to influence go uninfluenced. That means those people are more likely to stay small and stuck too. Stuck people stick people. (That's tweetable.)

This. Is. Why. You. Can't. Stay. Stuck.

But I've got great news for you. You don't have to stay stuck and overwhelmed and afraid forever. You have it in you to push your fear aside and do the big, hard, and scary things you were made for.

But you have to get unstuck first. So let's do it. Let's get you free. Your future is worth the fight. And so are you.

Know If You're Stuck

I want you to know there is so much hope. If you are stuck, scared, or overwhelmed and trapped in your own head . . . you are in the right place. And yes, girl, in case you aren't entirely sure, there is more for you. God does have more for you than this.

Jennifer Allwood

1

But are you *really* stuck?

You might not be.

Life is made up of seasons, and sometimes a season of rest can feel a little like being stuck if you're used to going a hundred miles an hour all the time. Or you may feel stuck because you've lost the forest for the trees, and if you pulled up to see the big picture, you'd realize just how much progress you're making. It could be that you are in the middle of a daunting situation that's so new and challenging that you feel stuck because you are moving slowly—but keep in mind, you *are* moving.

And moving *is* progress. And progress *is not* stuck.

So how can you tell if you're genuinely stuck or just unsure and overthinking things? Let's start with a little quiz to help you figure out where you stand. (Who doesn't love a quiz?)

And moving *is* **progress.**
And progress *is not* **stuck.**

Are You Stuck? Quiz

1. Is there a particular situation that has you feeling stuck?
   a) No
   b) Yes
   c) Yes—actually, there's more than one situation. Like, a lot of situations.

2. Is there an end date to whatever you're dealing with, such as a deadline or the end of a specific season or timeline?
   a) Yes, the end is in sight!
   b) No, but I really wish there were.
   c) It feels like it will always be this way.

3. Is the sticky situation something you can change or control in any way?
   a) Yes, but sometimes it doesn't feel like it.
   b) No, the only thing I can control is my attitude about it.
   c) Yes, I can control some of it, but not all of it.

4. Could you make a change today that would help, but you just haven't yet?
    a) Yes, but I just always feel so overwhelmed.
    b) No. If there were, I'd be doing it.
    c) I'm sure I could be doing something, but I have no clue what to do!

5. Are your feelings about your situation affecting other areas of your life?
    a) Yes, even though I've tried not to let it.
    b) Sometimes, but mostly not.
    c) Everything in my life always bleeds into everything else!

6. Do you feel hopeless and defeated?
    a) Yes, I am over everything.
    b) No, I still feel hopeful.
    c) My mood is basically just "Jesus, take the wheel."

7. Are you proud of how you've handled this situation?
   a) Not really.
   b) Mostly, yes.
   c) I'm not sure I've been proud of myself in a long time.

8. Are your stuck feelings affecting your family, coworkers, or friends?
   a) Yes, I'm sure they are. I'm not at my best.
   b) Mostly not.
   c) One-hundred percent, all the time.

9. Do other people think you are stuck?
   a) Maybe?
   b) No, but maybe a little overwhelmed.
   c) Of course they do!

10. Do you feel alive?
    a) I'm not sure.
    b) Yes, most of the time.
    c) I'm dead on my feet.

11. Do you feel joy?
    a) Sometimes, but it's been rare lately.
    b) Absolutely, just not all the time.
    c) Does awkward stress laughter count?

12. Do you look forward to your day?
    a) Some days more than others.
    b) Mostly, yes.
    c) I dread getting out of bed each morning.

13. Do you look at others with jealousy?
    a) When I'm feeling discouraged, yes. But not nearly so much when I feel good.
    b) Not often.
    c) All. The. Time. I need an Instagram intervention.

14. If you ask the people who know you best, would they say that you are stuck?
    a) Yes, although I've tried to hide it.
    b) No, I don't think so.
    c) No doubt.

15. Do you have a vision for your future?
    a) It's hazy.
    b) Yes, but how to make it come true has me feeling stuck.
    c) I can barely plan ahead to lunch, let alone the future.

16. Do you know in your heart that you were made for more, but for some reason, you just can't get over the hump to reach it?
    a) Can I get an *amen*? That's exactly how I feel!
    b) I know I was made for more, and I think I'm well on my way to getting there.
    c) Slow down with *made for more*. I'm just hanging on by a thread over here!

If you answered mostly *A*s, you are likely right on the line between struggling and stuck. The good news is that you don't have to lean toward the stuck side. There are things you can do to make sure you stay unstuck.

Mostly *B*s? I think you are just going through a rough patch. However, you know yourself best. If you feel deep down that you are stuck, you probably are.

If you answered mostly Cs, I just want to give you a big hug because, girl, welcome to Stuckville. I've been there. Let's get you out.

The good news is that it doesn't have to be like this forever. Friend, you can get unstuck. I pinky swear! The God of the universe is on your side and in your corner and partnering with you for a life that is wild and free. You are completely capable of having a life filled with peace and deep joy and expectancy.

A life without being stuck. A life without all the overwhelm. And a life where you have learned how to press forward amid fear.

This is a life worth living. Are you ready?

Getting to Know Yourself

As we get started, it's important to remember that the only person who can get yourself unstuck is you. So it's time to take stock of who you are and where you are right this minute. Today. Because if you don't know yourself or have been avoiding addressing different parts of yourself, then you are missing out on important information you'll need to move forward.

So let's get to know you, the *real* you. It's the best place to start when you're stuck.

Who Are You?

How would you describe yourself in five key words? Be kind. Be honest.

Ask some trusted friends too. What are the top words they would use to describe you?

What do you love most about yourself? Be braggy. It's okay.

_____

_____

_____

_____

_____

_____

What are your biggest strengths?

_____

_____

_____

_____

_____

_____

_____

What are your biggest weaknesses?

What is your favorite thing to do at work?

What is your least favorite thing to do at work?

What are your favorite tasks to do at home? Least favorite?

What is your favorite way to relax?

_____

_____

_____

_____

_____

_____

_____

How do you cope with stress in healthy ways?

_____

_____

_____

_____

_____

_____

_____

_____

How do you cope with stress in less healthy ways?

What are your three biggest priorities right now?

What are the three biggest changes you'd like to make in your life?

_____

_____

_____

_____

_____

_____

What do you want your life to look like in the next five years?

_____

_____

_____

_____

_____

_____

_____

_____

What are your biggest dreams—the ones you would regret forever if you didn't go after them?

_____

_____

_____

_____

_____

_____

Are you chasing them right now? How?

_____

_____

_____

_____

_____

_____

_____

_____

If not, why haven't you gone after them yet?

_____

_____

_____

_____

_____

_____

_____

Have you ever felt called to do something? If so, what was it?

_____

_____

_____

_____

_____

_____

_____

_____

Did you follow through with that calling?

Are you doing something right now that you feel called to do?

Is there something you've felt called to that you haven't done yet? Why not?

_____

_____

_____

_____

_____

_____

Do you believe you have a purpose? If so, what is it?

_____

_____

_____

_____

_____

_____

_____

_____

What are you doing right now to pursue your purpose?

What is helping you do that?

What is holding you back?

_____

_____

_____

_____

_____

_____

_____

Now that you've really explored who you are, it's time to delve into what you really want—for yourself, for your work, for your life. Are you ready?

What Do You Want?

I know all about delving into what you want. Let me tell you a story about how I figured this out for myself. One afternoon I was on a call with my business coach, Sandi Krakowski. Sandi was what my kids call "Facebook Famous," so I expected to discuss a new Facebook ad strategy with her, or how I should set up some sexy marketing funnel. But instead she told me that she had been praying about our coaching call and felt like she was supposed to ask me a question.

"What is it that you want?" she asked.

What the what? I froze.

What was it that I wanted? No one had ever asked me that before. Sure, I had been asked what I wanted for dinner and what I wanted for Christmas, but this was a much deeper, greater question. This was a "What do you want from life?" kind of question. And I, embarrassingly enough, had no idea.

> How could I *not know* at this point what I wanted from life?

I was fortyish when this happened. I know it sounds morbid, but for all practical purposes, I knew I was roughly halfway through my life. How could I *not know* at this point what I wanted from life?

The truth was, no one had ever asked me.

And the other more important truth was, I had never asked myself.

Just recently I discovered that even Jesus asked people what they wanted. "What do you want me to do for you?" (Matthew 20:32).

Whoa. I tried to imagine what would happen if it wasn't Sandi who asked me what I wanted, but Jesus. How lame would that be if I couldn't even come up with an answer for Jesus? *Not good, Jen, not good.*

Since that coaching call I have tried to determine what it is that I'm really hoping to get out of this one lifetime. Because we've gotta know where we want to go, friend. Or better yet, where God wants us to go.

So often, part of my being stuck was about my circumstances and my fear, but a lot of it was also my lack of vision. I had no idea where I wanted to go or what I wanted to do. And it's hard to leave a place you are stuck in emotionally or physically or spiritually if you have no idea where you are going *to*.

The truth is that no one can answer that question—*What do you want?*—except you. You are the only one who can find what God has called you to do. No one else can dive into your heart to discover your purpose. No one else can name your dreams and go after them. No one else can choose your priorities and honor them. No one else can cast a vision for what life should look like for you. God has gifted you with purpose, with opportunities, with passion and talents and strengths to make it all happen for *you*. He sets you in high places and gives you a seat at the table, but first you have to name what you want and commit to making it happen for yourself.

So let me ask you what Sandi asked me years ago:

What is it that you want? Do you know?

_____

_____

_____

_____

_____

_____

_____

_____

_____

_____

_____

It's okay if you don't know and have to leave that section blank. That's why I'm here—I want to help you figure it out.

Learning and Longing

Let's start by talking about the gazillion questions you answered a few pages back. Make sure you've answered them as honestly as possible. Now I want you to walk away and take a break. Not what you were expecting, right? But I'm serious. Take a walk or a nap or spend some time with your people. Or, if you're anything like me, treat yourself to a big bowl of chocolate chip cookie dough.

Then, in a couple of days, come back to this and read your answers again. Did writing that out help you see yourself a little more clearly? What do you think about the woman described in those pages? Do you like her? Are you proud of her? Do you think she's worthy of love and success and a meaningful life? Write down some thoughts you have about that woman.

Or are you comparing her to other women who seem to have it all figured out? You know the ones: the PTA mom who has never had to miss an event or maybe the friend with the amazing career you wish you had. The Instagram influencer always jetting off on enviable vacations or the down-to-earth celebrity you always secretly wished you were friends with. The woman in Bible study whose relationship with Jesus seems effortless and deep or even your bestie who is killing it with her business and whose marriage has never been stronger. Who comes to mind for you? Is there someone in particular? List her name below.

In what ways do you compare yourself to her?

More specifically, what does she have that you want?

_____

_____

_____

_____

_____

_____

You aren't alone in playing the comparison game. I don't think there's a woman alive who hasn't, at some point, compared herself to someone else and come up wanting. We all know we shouldn't, but sometimes we just can't help ourselves. Comparison really is the thief of joy, and it's also BFFs with stuck. Comparison and stuck: those two go together like macaroni and cheese.

Comparison and stuck: those two go together like macaroni and cheese.

The truth is, though, that comparison can also be one heck of a teacher when we're stuck. The jealousy or envy we feel toward someone else can help reveal our own deepest longings, especially when we're having trouble putting our finger on them.

For example, consider that PTA mom who has never had to miss an event. Deep down, you probably aren't jealous that she never misses a school event or meeting. Perhaps you're actually longing for a schedule that allows you to be more present with your kids. Or maybe you're dreaming of a life that isn't so busy and stressful.

Your focus on the friend with the amazing career may be revealing your longing for fulfilling work that matters to you. The Instagram influencer always jetting off to someplace new could be magnifying your longing for more adventure and excitement. Your desire to be closer to Jesus is probably what has you envying that woman in Bible study. And your bestie, killing it with her business and marriage? Well, if I were a betting girl (I'm not, but we can pretend!) I'd bet good money that you are longing to feel as free and unstuck as she seems to be.

Look back at what you wrote about who you compare yourself to and why. What might those answers be telling you about your longings?

If you are deeply longing for something and have no clear path to get there, that longing is basically a big ole arrow pointing right at where you might be stuck. Don't let that valuable insight go to waste. Drill down into it. Why are you longing for those things in particular?

What do you think would change if you were able to have those things?

The details of what He has planned for you won't be the same as what He has planned for someone else, but they will answer the specific longing in your heart

Whatever you're longing for, I want that for you. And that doesn't mean you have to feel guilty for wanting more. Wanting more isn't always a sign of discontentment. Sometimes we want more because we were made for more. And Luke 11:13 says that God wants those good things for you too. He made you with all the talents, passions, and gifts to go after everything your heart truly desires. He knows all about you—good, bad, and mediocre—and He's not comparing you to anyone else. So why are *you*? He's prepared good things for *all* His children, you included! The details of what He has planned for you won't be the same as what He has planned for someone else, but they will answer the specific longing in your heart. Trust that His plans for you are yours for the taking. You just need to get unstuck so you can find them.

Whose Are You?

Now that we know who you say you are and what you want for yourself, we've got a good starting point. But this section wouldn't be complete without figuring out who God says you are and what He wants for you because you will not get unstuck without God's help and without remembering His truth.

Before we move on, let's make one thing clear: God knows so much more than we do. He sees *everything*. Everything about you, about your situation, about your opportunities, about your entire life—every stinkin' second of it. So with that in mind, I trust Him and His opinions way more than I trust yours or mine.

When I am at my most stuck, it helps me to go back to my Bible and remind myself of who God says I am. Because—wow! He sees me so differently than I see myself, and that is such a wonderful, powerful, truly life-changing blessing. And the things He wants for me? Mind-blowing! You are so much more than you think, and there is so much more out there for you. God says so. And He is never wrong.

Who God Says You Are

- You are forever loved: Romans 8:38–39
- You are healed: Isaiah 53:5
- You are strong: Psalm 18:32
- You are forgiven: 1 John 2:12
- You are whole: Colossians 2:10
- You are never alone: Joshua 1:9
- You are filled with hope: Jeremiah 29:11
- You were created with purpose: Esther 4:14
- You are victorious: 1 Corinthians 15:57
- You will not be lost: Isaiah 30:21
- You are filled with peace: John 14:27
- You are joyful: John 15:11
- You are blessed and highly favored: Deuteronomy 28:13
- You are powerful, are loved, and have a sound mind: 2 Timothy 1:7
- You are fearfully and wonderfully made: Psalm 139:14
- You are valuable: Matthew 10:29–32
- You are worthy: John 3:16
- You are a beloved daughter: 2 Corinthians 6:18
- You are God's: Isaiah 43:1

Do you have any favorite verses you'd like to add here?

What God Wants for You

- God has plans for you: Jeremiah 29:11
- God wants to give you the desires of your heart:
  Psalm 37:4
- God wants to satisfy your desires, even in tough times:
  Isaiah 58:11
- God wants to teach you and watch over you: Psalm 32:8
- God wants to renew your strength: Isaiah 40:31
- God gives you a future and hope: Proverbs 23:18
- God created you for good works: Ephesians 2:10

- God wants to give you eternal life: John 3:16
- God gives you a purpose: Proverbs 16:3–4
- God wants to give you abundance: Ephesians 3:20
- God wants to light your path: Psalm 119:105
- God wants to make you brave: Deuteronomy 31:6
- God wants to set you in high places: Habakkuk 3:19
- God wants you to know the truth: 1 Timothy 2:4
- God wants to meet your needs: Philippians 4:19
- God gives you the ability to produce wealth: Deuteronomy 8:18
- God wants to bless you: 2 Corinthians 9:8
- God wants to give you a seat at His table: Ephesians 2:6

Use this space to add more as you discover what God wants for you!

Getting unstuck is learning to see yourself clearly, especially the messy stuff, so that you can pinpoint what has bogged you down and kept you small when you were made to be big.

Take the time to read over these verses—and reread them if needed. Highlight your favorites. Add them to your journal or your planner or your phone screen. Write them on your mirror in hot pink lipstick so you can't miss them when you are getting ready each morning. Memorize them and let them sink into your heart. Repeat them over and over until they become a part of you. Because one of the biggest parts of getting unstuck is believing—truly believing—that God's truth about you is greater than your ideas about you.

You don't need to be a new person. That's not what getting unstuck is about. God knows you and loves you just the way you are. Getting unstuck is learning to see yourself clearly, especially the messy stuff, so that you can pinpoint what has bogged you down and kept you small when you were made to be big.

Getting unstuck is digging deep to name the things you want for your life—the hopes, the dreams, the vision—so that you can start going for them. Getting unstuck is figuring out who you were made to be and with God's help bridging the gap between that version of you and the stuck version of you. You've got this.

Let's pray.

Father God,

I thank You so much for the truth You are revealing to me about myself and Your plans for me. Help me to see clearly and with Your wisdom who I am, and keep reminding me of whose I am. Stay by my side as I sift through my thoughts and feelings about myself to find the places where I have believed lies or have discounted something You have gifted me with. I want to honor You and Your creation of me by getting unstuck and living in Your freedom for me.

In Jesus' name, amen.

Know Why You're Stuck

Whatever you have been through and whatever people say to you, don't use it as an excuse. Use it as an incentive to get out and get on with your life.

Jennifer Allwood

Absolutely anyone can get stuck—you, your best friend, your mom, even the queen of England. Stuck doesn't just happen to the unlucky or the unmotivated or the unambitious. It happens to everyone. And it happens in many different ways and for many different reasons. If there were only one way to get stuck, it would be a heck of a lot easier to get unstuck, right?

Some of the things that have you stuck might be your own doing (at least a teeny-tiny bit), but a lot of them aren't. Either way, you need to know what is keeping you stuck before you can begin to unstick yourself. Even if you somehow manage to make progress, if you don't address the root cause, you will find yourself stuck again, over and over and over again. And no one has time for that. We want your unstuck to stick!

We want your **unstuck** to **stick!**

There are a lot of things in life that we didn't ask for, don't want, and would gladly return if we could. These are things in our past that we had no control over, yet they affected us just the same.

Some people inherit the feelings of being stuck, scared, and overwhelmed pretty much at birth from stuck, scared, and overwhelmed parents. Just as some people are born into and inherit wealth, you may have been born into and inherited struggle. It's important that you know that what has been passed along to you from your family is not your fault.

If you saw your parents unravel every time there was pressure in your family, you can't expect to know how to handle pressure any differently than how it was modeled for you. Right? If you saw one of your parents shut down and check out every time something difficult happened in life, that is the example you were handed.

We often behave like we were taught. But unfortunately we aren't always taught healthy, biblical ways of dealing with things. The good news is that you can relearn how to react. You can get free from being stuck.

What are those feelings, behaviors, and reactions you've inherited from the stuck people in your life?

_____

_____

_____

_____

_____

Who are the stuck people in your life? In what ways do they seem stuck?

_____

_____

_____

_____

_____

Do you think you are stuck in the same ways?

_____

_____

_____

_____

_____

_____

Are there any specific instances or patterns from your childhood that you find yourself repeating?

_____

_____

_____

_____

_____

_____

_____

If you could tell your past self anything, what would it be? What would you say to the version of you who didn't have a choice about where you were in life?

_____

_____

_____

_____

_____

_____

_____

_____

_____

_____

_____

_____

As adults we cannot continue to carry what others have put on us if we want to lead free lives. Even if you had a horrible experience or horrific childhood, you can blame your past for only so long and then it's time to take responsibility. You can't move forward until you leave your past behind.

I want to make it very clear that whatever generational junk you were dealt, you don't have to keep it, claim it, or pay for it any longer. What you were given does not have to be your handicap; but it *can* be your secret sauce if you choose to view it that way. Perception is a big part of this.

Even if you hate or were hurt by what was handed to you, you can still reframe it to see how it has helped make you the fighter you are today. If you were handed financial struggles, perhaps now you appreciate all you have in a big way. If you've grown up watching your mom make terrible decisions in relationships, well, hopefully now you have the gift of discernment.

> You can't move forward until you leave your past behind.

Look back at what you wrote for the last few questions. How can you reframe those struggles? Let's turn those into affirmations you can say whenever you need a reminder that you are getting unstuck from your past.

- I was handed _____ , so now I have _____ .
- I grew up with _____ , so now I know _____ .
- My family struggled with _____ , so I know the importance of _____ .
- I dealt with _____ , so now I fight to keep my life _____ .
- I could never have _____ as a child, and that taught me to _____ .
- I watched [FAMILY MEMBER'S NAME(S)] _____ struggle with _____ , so now I make sure to _____ .
- I make _____ a priority because of my experiences with _____ .
- I hated dealing with _____ in my past, so now I am careful to _____ .
- I am not [FAMILY MEMBER'S NAME(S)] _____ . I will not keep the [STRUGGLES] _____ I was handed.
- My struggles with _____ are not a handicap. They taught me to be _____ and that's my secret sauce!

Add your own reframing affirmations here.

Unfortunately, this stuckness doesn't just come from our past. What about the stuff others try to hand you *now*?

There will be people in your life—people you love, people who should be cheering you on—who will try their best to keep you stuck, sometimes without even realizing it. They are stuck too. Stuck people keep people stuck with them. They don't want you to change because it forces them to see that they should be digging deep and making changes as well. Even if they don't realize it, their fear causes them to say things to hold you back with them.

The truth is that those people's responses have very little to do with *you* and everything to do with *them*. You don't need to completely cut them out of your life, but those are not people you need to trust with your vision and plans.

I always tell my clients, it's not that those people are bad. It's just that they are bad for this season. They will try to crush your dreams and lead you off track. When you're working to get unstuck, stick with free people. Their freedom is contagious.

> When you're working to get unstuck, stick with free people. Their freedom is contagious.

If you've never seen a truly free woman, it's time to find one so you can see what unstuck really looks like. If possible, find one in real life, or even on social media. Study her. See how she rises above. Watch how she moves past fear and refuses to stay stuck. Observe how she handles things that would terrify you.

Who is your free-woman mentor?

What have you noticed about her that you are also doing?

What have you noticed about her that you aren't doing yet?

How can you start doing this?

_____

_____

_____

_____

_____

_____

_____

_____

_____

_____

_____

_____

I hate it that you may be surrounded by stuck people.

But whatever you have been through and whatever people say to you, don't use it as an excuse. Use it as an incentive to get out and get on with your life. Even though much of your being stuck may not be your fault, it *is* your responsibility.

And changing your mind is the first step to changing your life.

Let It Go

A huge part of changing your mindset is learning to forgive and let go. If you have been through something in your personal life that is making unforgiveness and bitterness an issue, those feelings will show up in other places—and not in a good way. Forgiveness doesn't mean that anything that happened to you was okay. Letting go of bitterness doesn't make a situation less unfair. But it does mean that it's over and not keeping you stuck any longer.

Think of a situation (or situations) in your life that you just can't get over. What is it?

Have you made attempts to forgive and move on? How did those attempts go? What happened?

_____

_____

_____

_____

_____

_____

Perhaps you have forgiven, but are you still bitter? When this situation comes up, does it give you a sinking feeling in the pit of your belly? When you see certain things or people on social media, do you feel triggered? Do you still feel a little hot all over at the very mention of their names? Share about that here.

_____

_____

_____

_____

_____

_____

Let's take a quick quiz, shall we?

1. Are you often jealous of the people around you who have what you don't?
   a) Yes, I want it all.
   b) Nope, I'm too blessed to be stressed.
   c) Sometimes, but isn't that normal?

2. Are you easily irritated by happy people who seem to have it all?
   a) Ugh. What are they so happy about anyway?
   b) No, I'm pretty happy myself.
   c) Mostly no, but *certain* happy people drive me nuts.

3. Do you criticize or gossip about people when they're not around?
   a) Only when someone is being annoying—which is always.
   b) I try really hard not to.
   c) Yes, but I never say anything I wouldn't say to their faces.

4. Does it ever seem like a person or a group is out to take things from you?
   a) They totally are, so yeah.
   b) No. There's enough for everyone.
   c) In certain circumstances, yes.

5. Is it difficult to trust friends and family who try to treat you well?
   a) Yes. If they're being nice they probably have an ulterior motive.
   b) No, they love me.
   c) Mostly no, but *certain* people can't be trusted.

6. Do you have trouble giving other people the benefit of the doubt when their words or actions are awkward?
   a) No one gives me the benefit of the doubt, so why should I give it to anyone else?
   b) No, I try to assume the best about everyone.
   c) Depends on how well I know them, I guess.

7. Do you have a difficult time apologizing when you're wrong, or congratulating and praising others when they do well?
   a) Yes. I know what I'm supposed to do, but I just can't get past my own feelings.
   b) No, not at all.
   c) Sometimes it's more difficult than others, but usually no.

8. Are you pessimistic about good news or new opportunities, always looking for the catch?
   a) My experience tells me that if it looks too good to be true, it probably is.
   b) No, I get excited and hopeful.
   c) I try not to be, but a tiny part of me can't help waiting for the other shoe to drop.

If you answered mostly *A*s, bitterness is a big problem for you and it's time to make like Queen Elsa and *Let. It. Go.*

If you answered mostly *B*s, you are in the clear! You have forgiven and moved on.

And if you answered mostly Cs, it sounds like you're dealing with a little bit of unforgiveness and bitterness, but you seem to be on the path to healing.

Regardless of how long you've held on to this situation, it's got to go. God has so much more for you if you will just let go of *that*. My pastor once told me that the worst thing I can give my children is a grudge. *Ouch!* That really resonated with me. I want to teach them to forgive, let go, and move on by my example. So I have to check my heart continually for bitterness. And if you're serious about getting unstuck and doing big things, you'll need to check your heart continually too. You do have a choice. You can move on. The decision is yours.

The next time that thing you've been holding on to pops back up (because it will; that's how bitterness works), say, "I've forgiven [insert name here]." Say it all day, over and over if you have to.

If someone else brings up the topic, change the subject.

If your thoughts start drifting that way, focus them on some of the good things God is doing in your life.

This **need** for forgiveness also means forgiving *yourself.*

If you continually do this, I promise that eventually your situation will stop having such a strong hold over you. You *will* find freedom from it.

And friend? This need for forgiveness also means forgiving *yourself*. Some of you have made bad decisions, done things you aren't proud of, hurt people, or [insert whatever thing you are ashamed of here]. And guess what? Me too. This is called being human. But if you've asked God to forgive you, it's already done. So if God forgives you, and as a Christian your call is to be more like Him, why are you not forgiving yourself? Share your thoughts here.

What do you need to let go of?

_____

_____

_____

_____

_____

_____

_____

_____

Who do you need to forgive?

_____

_____

_____

_____

_____

_____

_____

_____

_____

Let's get to it. Forgive. Let go. Because you have important work to do.

God needs you free to answer His calling for you.

Your spouse deserves you to be whole. Your kids need a healed mother. You deserve to get your headspace back so you can focus on what's important. God is offering you a holy exchange—your pain for God's plan. And that is one heck of a deal, my friend. *Take it.*

The Other Stuff

Generational junk, unforgiveness, bitterness—those are some majorly sticky things, right? Any one of them is enough to keep us stuck and struggling. But sometimes instead of one big thing, it's a combination of little things that keep us rooted in place. Things like guilt, indecision, imposter syndrome, confusion, perfectionism, and comparison. We *know* that those feelings aren't necessarily rooted in truth, but our feelings are big fat liars and they are very, very convincing. Once we start to believe those feelings, getting stuck is inevitable.

So many of these little things (the Bible refers to them as "little foxes") are fueled by social media. I've spent enough time

I've spent enough time online to understand that mindlessly scrolling through social media is killing more dreams and lives than people realize.

online to understand that mindlessly scrolling through social media is killing more dreams and lives than people realize.

When we are constantly bombarded with the best version of other people and then look at our own mess, of course we don't measure up. And those feelings of comparison and jealousy keep us stuck, especially since social media was designed to make you want more of it even when it makes you feel gross. Social media platforms are comparison traps. They make us feel guilty for the things we're not doing—and for a lot of the things we are. Every influencer tells us that she's got the solution to our problems, which just makes us more confused and indecisive. How can we make the right decisions when there are so many dang options? And even when we are proud of ourselves and happy with what we've accomplished, if we're constantly seeing women who are doing and achieving more it can make us feel like imposters.

Of course, we don't just look at other people on social media. We post also, and it's way too easy to become slaves to the selfie—putting out our own perfect images that make others feel as badly as we do! I am convinced that as a society, we've become more obsessed with *looking* happy on social media than actually *being* happy in real life.

There's a good reason the Bible tells us to "run with

perseverance the race marked out for *us*" (Hebrews 12:1, emphasis added). Because otherwise we would look around at all the other runners!

If you are constantly on social media, it becomes easy to question what you're doing and think it should be different or more. We aren't all called to run a business or travel the world or start a revolution, you know. Whatever you are being called to right now, don't let social media make you second-guess it.

Friend, you don't need to be intimidated or distracted by what anyone else is doing. You have the God of the universe to show you how to do it right. And guess what? The things He shows you won't look exactly like what anyone else is doing.

If you have a vision or a calling or a decision to make, a social media break may be just what you need so you are not influenced by anyone but God Himself.

Have Courage

When we feel confused and indecisive, guilty and dragged down by imposter syndrome, I'll tell you what we don't feel— courageous or confident. And that lack of confidence we think we *should* have definitely keeps us stuck.

Take a Break!

Take a social media break for two weeks. I double-dog
dare you! Track below how it makes you feel.

Day 1: _____

Day 2: _____

Day 3: _____

Day 4: _____

Day 5: _____

Day 6: _____

Day 7: _____

Day 8: _____

Day 9: _____

Day 10: _____

Day 11: _____

Day 12: _____

Day 13: _____

Day 14: _____

At the end of the two weeks, come back to answer
the following questions.

What did you miss most about social media?

What were you surprised not to miss?

Are there accounts you feel you need to unfollow after your break?

Over and over, I hear women say they are waiting to do things until they feel more confident. They think confidence is the magic, secret ingredient that will get them unstuck. And that, my friend, is nonsense. How can anyone expect to feel confident about something they've never done before?

The truth is that so many successful people aren't confident; they are courageous. They do things *in spite of* their low confidence level. Here's the thing: confidence is an end result of doing things while you're afraid. Confidence is what comes *after* you do the thing you're scared of—and then do the thing again, and again.

Confidence has to be earned. You can't buy it, manifest it, package it, or wish it into existence. The reason you're stuck isn't because you lack confidence. No, you're lacking the experience that will help you *feel* confident. There's such a huge difference.

It's time to **quit waiting** for confidence before you get out of your rut and out of your head.

It's time to quit waiting for confidence before you get out of your rut and out of your head. You don't need confidence. You just need the courage to say yes to something even with that nervous feeling in the pit of your stomach.

So now I have to ask: What have you been putting off doing or starting because you don't feel confident enough?

_____

_____

_____

_____

_____

_____

_____

When God has put something big on your heart, something you need to get unstuck to pursue, you don't need to feel confident to do it. You may not feel qualified, but you can be confident in the One who did the asking. God opens the doors, but we have to be courageous and obedient enough to walk through them. Whether or not we have confidence in ourselves is not even a factor.

If He is calling you *to* it, He will certainly call you *through* it. And you can have confidence in that! It's time to muster up the courage to do what God is asking you to do or what the desires in your heart are leading you toward.

What do you believe God is asking you to be courageous about today?

_____

_____

_____

_____

_____

_____

_____

_____

_____

_____

_____

_____

_____

The Bible tells us to recall and remember God's work, so let's do that! Think about all the times when God has come through for you in the past. Write them out below so you can come back to them and remind yourself of the times you acted even though you were scared and it turned out okay.

Own It

Change is possible, but it's entirely up to you. You—and you alone—are responsible for how you handle whatever you were handed in life and how you handle your emotions *today.*

Friend, whatever you do, the words you use, the thought patterns you play over and over in your mind—they matter.

You are a grown woman, capable of healing, being whole, doing hard things, and moving forward. But you must believe this to get unstuck. And you can't believe it if you keep reminding yourself of every mistake you've ever made. The reason we stay tied to excuses is

> Your feelings do not release you from your calling.

because we are scared. So we self-protect by making up all the reasons why we can't. It's time to stop letting those old missteps and excuses live rent-free in your mind.

God can fix bad thinking. He can help you overcome your feelings. Besides, your feelings about whatever you're trying to do in life, or whatever God is asking you to do, really don't matter anyway. (Since when did your *feelings* become a good reason not to do or try something?)

Your feelings do not release you from your calling. Your God-given calling is your purpose. It's the thing that makes you tick and that only *you* can do. It's your life's work. You will not be able to do it if you are going to choose to stay stuck with your fear.

You can't show up for God, for your husband, your family, the world, or your life if you continue to choose to stay tied to bad thinking, bad situations, and feelings that aren't true. It's up to you whether you stay stuck or move toward freedom. You can do this!

Let's pray.

Dear Lord,

I've been through some tough stuff and I've allowed it to keep me stuck, but I know You've always been there with me and that You are here with me now. Please keep showing me all the things and feelings and old wounds that keep me stuck. I want to name them so I can tackle them and work toward freedom. Please, God, help me do that. I know I can't do it all alone.

In Jesus' name, amen.

Plan to Become Unstuck

You owe it to yourself to show up for your life, and you owe it to your Creator to show up for the life He gave you.

Jennifer Allwood

It's time to make a commitment to yourself—right here, right now—to get unstuck. Getting stuck doesn't happen all at once, which means getting unstuck won't just magically happen all at once either. It will require you to work through all the junk that's been holding you back, replace some not-so-great habits with better ones, and get comfortable with being uncomfortable. No one ever said getting unstuck would be easy, but I can promise you that it will be worth it.

Still, because getting unstuck takes dedication, work, and facing down our fears and failures, it's a lot easier and more comfortable to stay stuck—even if that also means staying unhappy, unfulfilled, and uninspired. In other words, we can all be a little lazy. Motivation matters here.

Most people won't embrace change until they find the thing that is of greater importance to them than holding on to their fear and staying stuck. I call these "fear equations" and they are remarkably powerful—because I've found that the one thing that really moves the needle when it comes to getting unstuck is getting crystal clear on what is bigger than your fear.

Let's try it. First, think of the things that are most important to you in this life.

What matters more than your fear? What are the things that are greater than your staying stuck? What is more important to you than your feelings? Is it God? Your kids? Your marriage? Your friends?

_____ > my stuck
_____ > my fear
_____ > my feelings

_____ > my stuck
_____ > my fear
_____ > my feelings

Why?

_____

_____

_____

_____

_____

_____

You may have only one thing listed, or you may have ten. It doesn't matter as long as you can put a name to whatever is motivating you to become unstuck. I want you to write your fear equations and put them all over the place. On a sticky note on the dashboard of your car. Written in dry-erase marker on your bedroom mirror. Typed into a note you see frequently on your phone—heck, make that note your phone's wallpaper for a while! The goal is to keep reminding yourself of why the work you are doing to get unstuck is so vitally important.

Identifying *your* unique reason for getting unstuck is the first piece of the plan we're going to create to make long-lasting positive change in your life. This won't be a step-by-step plan, but more of a general plan of action designed to help you craft your vision for a life of freedom so you can make it a reality. When you know what you're working for, why you are working for it, and what you need to overcome, it's easier to identify your next best step and then the next best step after that. Change is tough, but so are you.

Motivation matters here.

If those things you wrote earlier *really* matter most to you, then you cannot stay stuck. You have to do the work to *show* that that is what matters most. You have to get unstuck.

Let God In

If you're convinced you need to do the thing you're scared to do, and if you're ready to get unstuck, the logical question that comes next is, *So what do I actually do?*

That feels like a daunting question, but it's ridiculously easy to answer. You simply ask.

If you don't know what you're supposed to do, you need to pray and ask God.

If you have no clue what you want to do, you need to pray and ask God.

If you are stuck, scared, or overwhelmed, or have any other issues keeping you down, you need to pray and ask God.

You do not have to do the work of getting unstuck all by yourself or all at once. What a relief! Here's the deal: God is waiting for you to take the steps required to heal and move forward, so you can start finding freedom for yourself. He is here to help, and I can promise you that working with Him will make this process so much easier.

Living life with God is not supposed to be you just sending up your laundry list of requests every week.

So ask Him for the answers you need. Ask Him for direction and vision and wisdom.

If you are already a prayer warrior who regularly hears from God, then this will be review for you. However, if you're like me, and learning to both pray *and* listen to God has been a learning process, then this section will be a huge part of your plan. Living life with God is not supposed to be you just sending up your laundry list of requests every week. That would be like my husband coming in, giving me a honey-do list, and then walking out before I could even respond. Wouldn't that be frustrating? That isn't a relationship with Jesus. That's a one-way transaction.

Have you ever heard from God? What did He say?

How did His answers change things for you?

_____

_____

_____

_____

_____

_____

_____

_____

_____

_____

God isn't a genie in a bottle or a teller at a drive-through window. He is our loving Father who wants to be an active part of our lives. It's time to deepen your relationship with God. It's time to look for God and really expect Him to show Himself to you. It's time to be still and listen, to have conversations with God, and to go from sometimes-prayers to a pray-hard revolution.

Figuring out what God wants will save you precious time, energy, and heartache. It's like having an unfair advantage and

He is the secret. I know from personal experience that one word from God can change everything. One idea from heaven can do more for you and your life in a hot minute than you can do in a decade.

If you haven't been much for praying in the past, that's okay. Start today, right where you are. God doesn't care if you get down on your knees or use fancy language. He just wants to hear from you and to share with you too. But the important thing is to ask God your question or what you need and then . . . well . . . shut up. Be still, listen, and wait. You can't hear from God if you don't hold space for Him to speak.

If hearing from God is hard for you, I want to share how you can listen for the sound of God's voice. For example, when I am stuck, scared, overwhelmed, or just needing to *hear* from God, I have to get away from the chaos of my life. I like to sit on our deck, but you need to find a place that feels right for you. Bring a notebook and a pen with you because you'll want to write down anything God tells you. Tell yourself (and anyone who needs you) that you are going to pray and you won't be back until you get an answer. Then pray.

I like to start out by thanking God for who He is and what He has already done because that's how prayer is modeled in the

Bible. Then I ask Him to remove any distractions. Next, I ask God a question and then sit quietly and wait for the answer, just as I would with my husband or my friends.

You should know that sitting and being quiet isn't natural for me. To ask the Lord a question and then sit there quietly waiting on an answer requires so much discipline. But if you can introduce this discipline into your life, *everything* will change. It's like having a GPS, a crystal ball, and a talent manager for your life when you ask God what you're supposed to do next.

I do think that sometimes people try to make the voice of God into this huge, distant, religious pie-in-the-sky thing, when really, it's the quiet voice in your head that's nudging you toward the thing you feel called to do but are scared to start. For me, God's voice is never loud. It's never shouting. It's never condemning. And once you begin to hear it, you *will* know it.

This is how I personally hear God. But God's voice to you might sound different. The cool thing about the God we serve is that He can't and won't be put into a box. So He will talk to *you* in a way that He knows *you* will best hear. Whatever the voice of God sounds like for you, my hope is that you will get really good at hearing it because the next step of your plan will be getting good at obeying His voice.

Is That My Voice or God's?

This is a tough one, huh? When I really want something, it can be easy to trick myself into believing that it's something God also wants for me without even realizing I'm doing it. Sound familiar?

Luckily there are some ways to double-check myself to make sure I'm listening to God and not my own ego or ambition.

- If it's smarter than anything I could come up with, it's God. For real. He will tell me to say something or do something that I would never come up with on my own.
- If it's something that I know is the right thing to do, but I just don't want to do it, it's God. For example: Take off my headphones and actually talk to the person next to me on the plane. Call my mom even though I don't have time. Return the shopping cart to the cart corral.

- If I just can't stop thinking about something that's scary or challenging or big, it's God.

- If it's something that aligns with Scripture, it's God. He will never tell you something that goes against what's in the Bible.

- And if God is silent? He's probably still waiting for me to do the last thing He told me. Or He's teaching me to trust that He'll deliver the answer in His own timing. Or maybe He's even asking me to open up my blind eyes to see what He's already doing. Or perhaps it's a question that He wants me to decide upon—because He does let us decide plenty.

- Sometimes God speaks to us almost audibly, and other times it's more of an intense gut feeling.

Before you plan anything else, start praying. Ask God questions about your life and your future. Ask Him to show you your purpose. Ask Him to lead you to the people you need to learn from. Then listen. Be patient. Not every answer will look or sound the same. So listen for words or for an internal nudge that pushes you in a certain direction. Talk to Him every day, every hour, until you get the answers you need to move forward.

Write your prayers and answers here.

Come back to this section and add more prayers and answers as you move forward. Watch and see what happens in this section as you fill it up with direction from God. You'll begin to see glimpses of the bigger picture, the life that's waiting for you when you get unstuck.

If you're stuck, He has the answers.

If you're overwhelmed, He has the relief for that.

If you're scared, He has the voice of reason that you need.

Ask Him, and then listen and watch for Him.

Once you begin to hear from heaven, it changes everything.

Say Yes

The next part of the plan to get unstuck is to start saying yes. When you feel that pull or that little internal nudge that you know comes from God, say yes. Even when it's awkward or uncomfortable or inconvenient. Because remember, you aren't just getting unstuck for yourself. We were all created to live more for God and for others than we were for ourselves. God has a plan for you and your life—a much bigger and better plan than anything you and I can come up with—and He already knows you have what it takes to see that plan through.

There is something comforting about knowing someone smarter than me already has it figured out. I just have to keep saying yes as the plan is presented to me. And not "Yes, but maybe later in a month when things slow down," or "I'll do that next year when the kids are older." God expects a yes immediately.

> **If you stay stuck, things are not getting accomplished on this side of heaven in the time that they may need to.**

You have a responsibility to Him, to your family, to yourself, and to the world. I don't know about you, but every plan I've ever made has a schedule or time frame attached to it. So when God says He has plans for us, I can safely assume that those plans are time sensitive. I like to imagine God with His day planner patiently but pointedly waiting on me to get a move on. God is loving, patient, and kind, but He is still God. He has things that need to get done on this earth. And it's in our best interests to get on board, and on time, with His plans. If you stay stuck, things are not getting accomplished on this side of heaven in the time that they may need to. This can affect so many people. There is a ripple effect.

If you stay stuck, who will it affect?

_____

_____

_____

_____

_____

_____

_____

_____

If you ignore the purpose God has entrusted to you, who will you let down?

_____

_____

_____

_____

_____

_____

_____

_____

_____

God doesn't want our excuses; He wants our yes. He wants us to trust that as our Father in heaven, He has a different vantage point than we do. We may not understand why He is asking us to do certain things, but He hopes we trust Him enough to just do it.

At the end of the day, who has authority in your life? Who are you trusting?

Do you really deep down believe that the God of the universe has good things for you? And that to access those things fully, you have to be obedient even if it scares you?

God has so much He wants to partner with you on, but you have to be free in order to do that. You owe it to yourself to show up for your life, and you owe it to your Creator to show up for the life He gave you.

What are the big things God is asking you to do?

No Excuses

When you think about the big things you're being called to do or create or change, are those thoughts immediately followed by a laundry list of excuses for why you can't possibly do them? I'm almost certain they are. Write out all your excuses below:

We all have excuses, but moms are especially susceptible to finding a million reasons to put things off. As a mom, I have so much going on that there is always another excuse locked and loaded, another reason why now isn't the best time or why something isn't possible, especially since I'm so focused on taking care of everyone else in my family.

Have you ever noticed how quickly our kids can push our buttons? How easily they can wound us because they know our weak spots? How quick they are to notice when something is wrong?

Our kids know us way better than we give them credit for. When it comes to doing the big, hard, scary things in life, it will often be our children who know if we are stalling or if our talk doesn't line up with our walk.

Kids will call our bluff from a mile away.

Mom, you are the example your kids need to see of how to get unstuck, stay unstuck, and live free. Who else on this side of heaven will teach them that? And the truth is, they will have times in their lives when circumstances or events or feelings try to keep *them* stuck. You want them to be able to remember how you handled those times so they have a godly example to go by.

When it comes to doing the big, hard, scary things in life, it will often be our children who know if we are stalling or if our talk doesn't line up with our walk.

Part of the reason this whole getting unstuck thing is hard for women is that we tend to put ourselves last on the list, especially if we are wives or mothers. But I want you to remember, friend, that you were someone before you were anyone's wife or mom, and that person still matters.

If God is asking you to do big, hard, scary things in addition to raising kids, take heed. Don't use those babies as an excuse to delay. He is fully capable of taking care of *them* while you take care of *that*. But every *yes* you give to something else means you are saying a *no* at home, so it's imperative that you are not doing what *you* think you should do but rather what *God* says to do.

And so I challenge you to look at yourself through the eyes of your kids. What do they see? Would they say "my mom is brave"? Would they say "my mom is obedient to God"? Would they say "my mom does hard things"? Go ask them.

What words did they use?

Take a good look at that list of excuses you wrote. If God was standing in front of you right now asking you to step up, get unstuck, and fulfill the purpose He has created just for you, would you actually hand God any of those excuses? I don't think so. But that's exactly what we do every day when we use those same excuses to stay stuck and small.

But if we're going to change our future, we have to quit looking to other people . . . to do the job that God has given *us* to do.

God has anointed His daughters and equipped His girls, and He fully expects us to rise up. He is raising up a group of women who are not just hearers of the Word; they are doers as well (James 1:22). But if we're going to change our future, we have to quit looking to other people (our spouses, our bosses, our coaches) to do the job that God has given *us* to do.

Oh girl, I hope you just heard that.

If you are broken, you are a solution.

If you are unhappy, you are a solution.

If you are stuck, you are a solution.

God has equipped *you*, friend. He has given *you* dreams. He has given *you* ideas. He has given *you* things that only you can do in the world. And your saying yes to those things even if you are scared, even if you feel stuck, even if you have a million excuses, is what will change your family and change your life. If you are stuck and overwhelmed, I am telling you to ask God what *you* could do or should do to help your family.

Friend, it's time to break this bad excuse habit. Go back to that list of excuses you wrote a few pages back. In the "No Excuses" column I want you to write a counter to each excuse. Make your counters as personal and specific as you can. Of course, if you can't think of something specific, it's perfectly fine to write "My kids need to see me get unstuck," or "God needs me free to fulfill my purpose."

Every time you reach for one of your old excuses, have your counter-excuse ready. Turn those counters into affirmations that you repeat to yourself every day. Keep reminding yourself of why those excuses don't have a hold on you anymore and eventually you'll stop making them altogether.

You have a plan in place now and are prepared to deal with being stuck, right? Okay, all that's left is to actually unstick.

Let's pray.

Heavenly Father,

Thank You for opening my eyes to all the ways my thinking and habits have been keeping me stuck. Thank You for having bigger, better plans for my life than all that. I'm ready to get unstuck. Please keep reminding me that this is worth fighting for when I start to get a little lazy about it. I want to be ready to embrace Your plans for me, and I know I have to get unstuck to do it. I'm ready!

In Your Son's name, amen.

Unstick

If a woman can change her mind, she can change her life.

Jennifer Allwood

Alright, friend, we've made it to the point where it's time to put your money where your mouth is and unstick. This will require you to step beyond the planning stage and actually get to doing.

Dreaming is great, but the *doing* is what matters.

Do what you're scared to do. Do what needs to be done. That is the real secret to unsticking. Doing is what will propel you out of stuck and into something far better. Friends, *it is time*.

> Dreaming is great, but the *doing* is what matters.

Right here I want you to write down everything you can think of that you need to do to get unstuck.

_____

_____

_____

_____

_____

_____

Do you have anything on your list that includes journaling, reflecting, brainstorming, or setting intentions? If so, cross those things off. There is a time and place for those things, but that time and place was the last three sections. Now it's time to start.

Plenty of women have died with a journal full of goals and intentions and dreams, with none of them realized on this side of heaven. You cannot continue to pray and pray and pray, asking God to make a way when you refuse to take a step. You cannot ask God to show you what He wants you to do if you've been ignoring what He's been whispering in your ear for years. You can't expect God to give you the full picture when you won't even do the *next thing* He's asking you to do.

What will you commit to doing today?

_____

_____

_____

_____

_____

_____

_____

I know it's scary to start. What if you do the wrong thing?

I promise that even if the first step you take is a disaster of a wrong choice, it will be okay. At least you're starting. God is fully capable of fixing any and every mistake. As long as you are in motion, He can reroute you, pull you back, bypass a misstep, and switch your direction. But even God cannot steer a parked car.

Don't let the start stop you.

Yes, it may be clumsy. Yes, it may not be the best work you ever do. Yes, you may look like a newbie. But you will be doing it and that is what matters.

The kind of life you long for doesn't come by playing small. It comes from getting in the game. It comes from deciding to *do* something today that will take you one step closer—and then having the courage to keep going.

And that, my friend, is a life worth living.

Don't let the start stop you.

The Next Best Step

Repeat after me: *I do not have to do it all today.*

Say that as many times as you need to in order to let that truth sink down into your bones. Even God did not create *everything* in one day. He did it over six days, and He is infinitely more powerful than you and me. Which means that no matter how hard you try, you cannot create the life you want right this minute.

We often stop ourselves at the beginning because we're not sure where we will end up or how long it will take us to get there, and that can feel frustrating and overwhelming. We live in a world that prioritizes instant gratification. We all want what we want when we want it (which is usually yesterday!), so it makes perfect sense that starting something big and uncertain freaks us out a little. But honestly, sometimes ignorance is bliss.

I believe with my whole heart that it's because of God's goodness that He doesn't show us the whole picture or give us the whole plan in advance. I bet it would intimidate the heck out of us.

If God hasn't given you the whole picture yet, count your blessings. We can't handle the whole picture. It's better to see only the next step and not absolutely everything that's coming our way. This allows us room to grow and evolve without the pressure of an end result or an end date. Don't stress that you don't know where you're headed. You know the One setting your course and you can trust His navigation system.

So stop looking ahead. You don't have to know what's a mile or five or ten down the road. All you have to do is take that first step. And then take the next obedient step after that. And then the next. Don't stop. Don't second-guess yourself. Just keep stepping and trusting God to direct those steps to where they need to go. Eventually, if you keep right on taking the next best step, you will find yourself five or ten miles down the road and be truly amazed at how far you've come.

I know taking those first few steps can be daunting. But it's not as difficult as we make it out to be. Most of the time, we just need twenty seconds of dig-down-deep courage. It takes only twenty seconds to dial that number or send that email or press submit on that application. Twenty seconds is *nothing*, my friend. It takes me longer to put on my mascara every morning. Even if you are sweating through your shirt and shaking in your sneakers, you can be brave for twenty seconds to take that step.

What step can you take today with twenty seconds of insane courage? Can you do it right now?

What about tomorrow? The next day? Next week? Write down one courageous thing to do every day for this week and next. Then do them.

How did it feel to take that step?

Did all your worst fears come true?

What actually happened?

You've got the courage inside you to start. Once you do, God will come alongside you to bring you exactly to where He wants you to be. He will make a way, even in the wilderness, when you get on board with what He wants. Remember, friend, if you said yes to God, you said yes to *His* plan. But you will never know what that looks like until you take the first step.

So What?

Unsticking may require you to get comfortable with being uncomfortable. Getting unstuck may not be a straightforward process. You may take two steps forward and one step back. You may fail and try again and fail and try again. You may feel embarrassed or awkward or exhausted and want to give up. Even though this is normal, it doesn't make it any easier.

Fear is *not* the boss of you.

Embarrassment, awkwardness, shame—all these emotions are rooted in fear. Fear can be a big, intense feeling—but it is still *just* a feeling. You are a fully grown woman and you aren't going to let your fear or your feelings control you. Fear is *not* the boss of you.

It is absolutely okay to be scared. It's absolutely okay to acknowledge that you're scared. Let yourself feel the fear. Denying your fear won't help you any more than letting your fear carry you away.

Fear is actually useful at times. We *should* be scared if we come face-to-face with a grizzly bear or get too close to the edge of that drop ten stories down. Fear in those situations could save our lives. God wired your brain to feel fear to protect you.

But interviewing for a better job or launching a business or asking for a raise? Unless that better job is with the CIA, it's unlikely any of those things will kill you. In those cases, instead of saving us, fear slows us down and locks us up. Your brain just can't discern when healthy fear is needed and when unhealthy fear will make things harder.

So be scared. And then move on.

This is real life, and we have to discover a deep conviction that, yes, hard things are hard. But fear cannot stop us from doing what we want and what we are supposed to do. You're scared. I'm scared. We're all scared. But if you feel God nudging you, encouraging you, wanting you to start the business, make the call, have the talk, then your fear isn't even a factor to consider. And the only way to fight that fear is by *doing the thing that scares you.*

Friend, fear can take you for a ride on the crazy train. It can take a normally rational woman and break her down with that wild, worst-case-scenario, unhinged voice straight from her anxious imagination. Fear is not logical. I've gotten much better at pushing my fear (and that voice!) aside because I know that none of that is God's best for me. But that fear didn't just go away on its own. I've gone through therapy. I avoid watching shows and movies or reading books with plots that tie into my worst fears. And I remind myself every time that little voice surfaces—ready to tell me that we all might go down in flames—*Even if that happens, it's going to be okay because I have survived every bad situation up until now.*

I am tough, and I've survived a lot of things I really believed might just do me in. Every single time God was with me, protecting me, and carrying me through. My fear did not manage to call down the worst of the worst on my head, and yours hasn't either. If it had, you wouldn't be sitting here today reading this book.

Think of the worst thing you've ever been through.

Did you survive it?

What did you learn from it?

_____

_____

_____

_____

_____

If you survived *that,* you can absolutely survive *this.* Still not sure? Okay, well, the next time you step out to do something big and scary, even if it fails miserably, what's the worst that could happen?

_____

_____

_____

_____

_____

_____

What would you do then?

If you're thinking about the thing that you feel you should do, and that God is calling you to do, but you feel stuck because of fear and what-ifs, can you get to the heart of the issue? *If x happens . . . then I will y.*

And if y happens . . . then I will z. And if z happens . . . then it will suck, but I will make it. See how that works? Just voicing those possibilities can help you calm down and see your situation with a slightly different perspective.

Now ask yourself, "So what if I succeed? What's the best that could happen?" and then answer that question too. Drill it down. *If x happens . . . then I will y. And if y happens . . . then I will z. And if z happens . . . then it will be amazing, and I will celebrate big time.*

The truth is that very, very, very rarely is the worst case that you will die or be financially wrecked or somehow ruin your life. Usually, the worst-case scenario is embarrassment or awkwardness or a blow to your pride. And while those things aren't exactly comfortable, they are never a reason not to do something. I've left some space here for you to try this out for yourself a few times.

What do you feel anxious about?

So what if you fail?
What's the worst that could happen?

What would you do then?
So what if you succeed?
What's the best that could happen?

What would you do then?

What do you feel anxious about?

So what if you fail?
What's the worst that could happen?

What would you do then?
So what if you succeed?
What's the best that could happen?

What would you do then?

The truth is, even if the very worst thing happens, you *will* survive. You have survived every awful thing in your life up till now, which makes the statistics of your surviving the next bad thing pretty doggone high.

Living "safe" is a fantasy. But living in God's plan and knowing that the God of the universe is right there with you if things don't go right? Well, that's the best place to be. But—and this *but* is *so* important—many other times you will succeed. And that success will be even better and sweeter than you can imagine. Don't let the fear of failure stop you from having the chance to succeed. You deserve that chance.

Fear is a muscle that you train, and you can train yourself to do things while scared. How? By doing things that make you scared over and over and over and providing yourself with the evidence that you are fully capable of doing hard things.

So you're scared? So what? Me too. So is that girl over there. And her. We're all scared.

So just take the first step. Oh, you're scared again? Just take the next best step. And the next and the next, until you string together a life made up of times you did great things regardless of how you felt.

Just take the next best step. And the next and the next, until you string together a life made up of times you did great things regardless of how you felt.

Stay on Task

One of the biggest roadblocks to getting unstuck is that it can be tough to stay the course. Once you get a few steps in, everything can suddenly feel extra messy and confusing—they don't call it the *messy middle* for nothing!

The messy middle of any project or situation is often what separates the women from the girls, when the excitement has worn off and now you've just gotta do the work.

Frustration pops up. The work is mundane. It's drudgery. Sometimes it feels like swimming upstream. It's easy to get distracted or want to give up in that stage, but don't give in. Instead, work with your natural inclinations to stay on task.

Once you have a plan, you simply have to keep going through the steps. Yes, it may take time and for sure it will take energy, so make it as easy on yourself as you can. We're all wired to be more productive at certain times and in certain places. Lean in to those tendencies. If you're a night owl, set aside a few hours in the evening to work on your plan. An early bird? Set that alarm and get stuff done before the day starts for the rest of your family.

What time of day do you work best?

_____

_____

Where do you work best? A silent office or a bustling coffee shop? On your deck or lounging on the sofa?

_____

_____

How can you optimize your unsticking time to work best for when and how you work best?

_____

_____

_____

_____

_____

_____

_____

This might feel counterintuitive because as women we're used to doing this all the time, but resist the urge to multitask. Focus on one task at a time. Complete that and then move on to the next. When you split your focus and ping from task to task, you can't get in the zone, which is where the magic happens.

When you can get in a flow with your work, where everything outside of the work fades away, you will find yourself working and creating and problem-solving at a higher level. But if you're being interrupted every ten minutes, it's almost impossible to stay in that flow zone.

Resist the urge to multitask.

When you get into that flow, it will help you to batch your work. If you need to create ten blog posts for your website for the next ten weeks, you don't have to write one each week. If your writing is flowing, write multiple posts in one afternoon and then just post one a week. Or how about dinner? You know you need to cook dinner every night, right? Take an hour or two to chop all the veggies you'll need for the week and put them away, ready to go. It will be much faster than cutting veggies every single night.

When possible, plan ahead to group similar tasks together. I promise you will complete them much faster in one go than if you sat down at multiple times to do the same tasks.

Which tasks that you do frequently can you batch together?

It matters to God how we're using our time. We get only so many hours in each day and we don't want to waste precious afternoons and mornings for nothing. Getting unstuck is 100 percent worth your time, but it doesn't have to take forever either. Finding ways to be your most efficient is part of being a good steward of the time you've been given, and it will help you get unstuck faster, which is a win-win for everyone. Of course, even at your most efficient, you won't have time for everything, which brings us to our next section.

Get Help

Getting unstuck is certainly your responsibility, regardless of your fear and uncertainty, but that doesn't mean you have to do it alone. None of us is an island, and we all need other people on our team to support us, encourage us, and yes, sometimes lend us a helping hand. Your husband, your mother or mother-in-law, your babysitter, and your friends are all on your team, so use them!

Your team cannot do the work for you, but they sure as heck can make the work easier. Women so often believe that we have to do everything ourselves. But that is nonsense. No one can possibly do everything. Even the Proverbs 31 woman had maidens to help her out! So, yes, you are allowed to ask for help—guilt-free. You absolutely can do *anything*, but you can't do *everything*.

One thing I see over and over that slows down women who are trying to unstick is that they think they need to keep everything in their lives in balance. But the Bible doesn't once tell us to pursue balance. Instead, we are called to pursue peace. And being stuck is not peace.

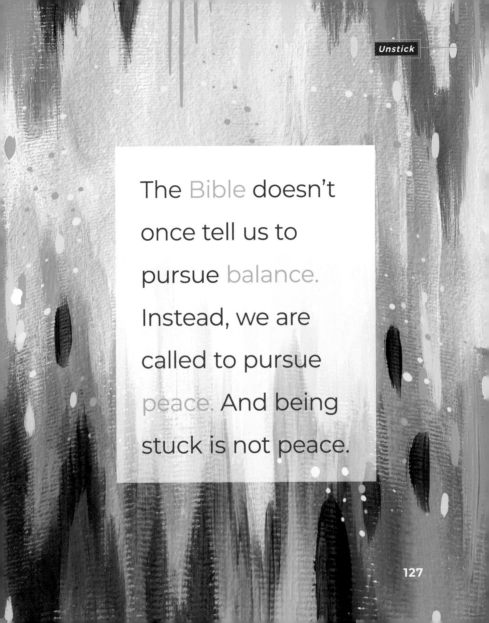

The Bible doesn't once tell us to pursue balance. Instead, we are called to pursue peace. And being stuck is not peace.

Getting unstuck will require you to give it your all, which means you will probably have less time for other things for a while. This is not forever. This is a season where you sacrifice a little *there* to gain a lot over *here*. I promise that your family and friendships will survive, and, what's more, they will be better able to thrive when you are unstuck and thriving.

The answer is simple: make more time by learning to leverage it. This is where your team comes in, and where you may have to invest a little extra money in yourself. Ask for help. Can your husband do all the cooking for a few weeks (or all the time, like mine)? Or can you expand your budget to include more convenience foods? Will your mother-in-law come by for after-school care for the kids? Or can you arrange childcare with a neighbor, knowing you'll help her out the same way next month? Can you pay a little extra to order groceries online? Is it possible to arrange for a laundry service for the next month? Do you need to hire an assistant or a consultant to teach you something you've been struggling to learn?

How can you find more time to unstick?

Who can you ask for help? Who is a part of your team?

Asking for help does not make you weak or incapable. It makes you human. It's not selfish to prioritize making the moves that will bring you and your family more freedom. It's not self-indulgent to want to pursue what God is calling you to. You do not need to feel guilty for wanting a life brimming with purpose and conviction. It's actually brave and obedient, and you are setting a wonderful example for the people in your life. You've got this!

Let's pray.

Father God,

Please help me to take my first step to unstick myself. Thank You for having a vision of my future that is so much bigger than my own. Do what You need to do to prepare me for that future. Make me into who I need to be to handle what You have for me. I want to be who You need in every way. I want Your plan, Your timing, Your purpose for my life, and I know I can trust You not to give my family and me more than we are ready for. In Jesus' name, amen.

Stay Unstuck

You are 100 percent, no joke, completely and utterly made for this.

Jennifer Allwood

Freedom is a beautiful feeling. When you finally unstick and get to revel in being free, believe me, you will always want to stay that way—and I want to help you do exactly that. I don't want you to fall back into that mess of exhaustion, overwhelm, confusion, indecision, and perfectionism. Yuck! So let's talk about how to stay unstuck!

Just like getting stuck doesn't just happen one day, staying free doesn't just happen either. You must work at it. You must be vigilant to avoid sliding back into old habits and patterns that kept you stuck in the first place. That means you must keep doing the hard things. Keep facing down your fears. Keep working through all the junk you were handed from your family or childhood. Keep slaying your dragons. Keep praying. Keep listening to God, and keep saying yes to what He asks of you.

> Just like getting stuck doesn't just happen one day, staying free doesn't just happen either.

God wants you to be His yes-girl. Your husband may need you to step up and help be the solution to your family's problems with money, parenting, relationships, or anything else—they are half yours, right? Your kids need to see you living as a free woman so they know what that looks like and so they know freedom is possible for them too. The world needs you free and running with everything you have after your purpose, lighting things up like only you can.

Everyone around you benefits when you remain free, and everyone around you misses out when you get stuck.

Do it for God.

Do it for your people.

Do it for yourself.

Let's go!

Resistance

It would be so nice to be able to tell you that once you are unstuck and moving it will be nothing but leisurely days filled with champagne, confetti, and ice-cream cake, but nothing could be further from the truth.

There is an enemy of your soul who wants you stuck. He wants you broken. And he is going to throw a fit when you get unstuck and do what God is asking you to do. The bolder you become, the more you are pressing toward what God has for you on this side of heaven, the more pushback you are probably going to get. This is resistance.

Resistance is when things get hard because it will feel like everything is going against you.

The more stuck you used to be, the more resistance you'll face.

The bigger the call on your life, the more resistance you'll get.

The greater the impact you are about to have on people, the more resistance you may encounter.

Maybe you can relate. Imagine you're on a roll with what you're doing when suddenly the car breaks down or the dishwasher floods your kitchen or the hot-water heater breaks. Then one of the kids gets the flu and the other tells you he's failing math and needs extra help. Then your husband has to travel for work, so it's all on you to handle all of the above plus the dog's annual vet visit and all the brownies that have to be baked for the PTA bake sale. Whew!

Nothing like a whole mess of distractions to make sure you have zero time to keep going with your calling. This is resistance. When this happens to you, take a few deep breaths and remind yourself that this is happening because you are on the right track. It doesn't make those things any easier to deal with, but it can have a big effect on your attitude.

Distraction is one of the Enemy's most-used forms of resistance because it's so dang effective! A pastor I know has said that if the Enemy can't discourage you, he will do his best to distract you. The enemy of your soul will distract your mind to keep you from doing what you should do. It's pathetic how much he does it and how often we fall for it. No one, and I mean no one, is exempt from the resistance of distraction.

But distraction isn't the only kind of resistance. Resistance can look like pushback. Like when you can't get your license or permit approved or you have to redo your application because it was rejected *again*. Your shipments are all delayed or every activity or class you wanted to sign your kids up for is full. It can be so frustrating.

Resistance doesn't just come through situations. It can also come from the people who are closest to you. People who don't catch your vision and make you feel small and vulnerable with their comments and teasing. People who tear your ideas down instead of encouraging you to keep trying. Most of the time these people don't realize how much they're hurting your feelings and messing with your head, but that doesn't make it any easier to deal with.

Resistance can also look like procrastination. I'm most

Friend, if you are waiting for it to be perfect, you're making an excuse and you are putting off until tomorrow what might already be good enough today.

vulnerable to the resistance of procrastination when I feel extra vulnerable about what I'm doing. It's a heck of a lot easier to scroll Instagram than it is to dig deep. It's more fun to complete a small project for an easy win than it is to keep plugging away at the big one stretching out in front of you. But choosing the fun, easy thing now will always catch up with you later, and you'll pay a price.

Procrastination is BFFs with perfectionism, which is another sneaky form of resistance that can really derail us if we let it. We convince ourselves that we'll just hold off until we're "ready." We decide to wait until we can produce something that's perfect. But ready is a lie, and perfect is impossible. No one is ever completely ready.

The truth is that the first step doesn't need to be perfect. Perfectionists are just as scared as the rest of us, but somehow the idea of waiting until things are perfect *sounds* honorable. Trust me when I say perfectionism is a sticky trap you need to avoid. Let's go with progress over perfection. "Good enough" instead of redoing it for the tenth time. Done and sold instead of still tinkering and not even on sale. Friend, if you are waiting for it to be perfect, you're making an excuse and you are putting off until tomorrow what might already be good enough today.

Doubt is its own sticky form of resistance. That's when you let your mind revisit every single time you've messed up in the past. You tell yourself that since *that* didn't work then, *this* won't work *now*, never mind that you've learned and grown and changed your approach based on your past failures. Never mind all the other successes you've had, all the times when what you tried did work! These are the same doubts that had you stuck before. They didn't disappear just because you pushed past them—no, that would be too easy. You will face these same doubts about yourself and your abilities over and over, no matter how successful you become because the Enemy knows how easily we crumble under the weight of our own doubt and insecurity.

Remember, the Enemy wants to discourage you. He knows that when a woman obeys God and sticks with it and does what she knows she should, she is a force to be reckoned with.

So, I want you to anticipate resistance. Don't be shocked when life seems to push back. Instead, remind yourself that resistance means you are on the right path and you need to keep going. Take it as the compliment it is. You, free and pursuing your purpose with God, are armed and dangerous in the eyes of the Enemy. You are a fighter, a warrior, a spark waiting to set the world on fire for God.

Are you willing to go to battle with the Enemy for what
you want for you and your family?

_____

_____

_____

_____

_____

_____

Which form of resistance are you most vulnerable to?

_____

_____

_____

_____

_____

_____

How can you guard against resistance? Or keep it at bay?

_____

_____

_____

_____

_____

_____

How will you handle it when it pops up? Brainstorm some ideas here.

_____

_____

_____

_____

_____

_____

_____

_____

Resistance will often come when you start something new. It will haunt you through the messy middle. And it will ramp up whenever you're about to level up. It could be hard. It's supposed to be. If it weren't hard, everyone would be doing it. And the devil doesn't bother opposing things that don't matter. What you are doing *matters*. I believe it counts toward eternity.

Doing what God asks you to do, living in your purpose, and walking in your calling *will* be hard. Being obedient will be hard. But watching your purpose pass you by because you were too scared to step into it . . . that may be even harder.

Regret is hard.

It's all hard. It's supposed to be. So pick your hard.

I pray you pick wisely. I'm rooting for you.

Get Organized

One big way to push back against resistance is to commit to moving forward. You have to keep identifying the next best step and taking it or you will find yourself stuck again, back in the muck of chaos and confusion.

Chaos happens when we have too much going on with no system for how to handle it, which always leads to confusion. It's impossible to be productive when your life is in chaos. You'll find yourself spinning in place like a top.

When you get confused you'll find yourself unable to stick to one idea or one project, jumping from thing to thing without finishing anything. You might have a lot of options, ideas, and strengths, and that is a good thing, but it means you'll have to focus and take action to gain clarity and make choices for yourself.

Confusion becomes clarity when you start listening to that still, small voice inside that is the Holy Spirit—when you start making decisions for yourself with God. Confusion becomes clarity when you take responsibility for the chaos and take steps to get organized and focus.

What are you avoiding taking a hard look at? Avoiding those things keeps you in confusion. Attacking it head-on will give you clarity. You can't start to understand things if you don't bring them into the light and look at them. Once you do, then you can organize a plan of action to tackle the chaos and restore clarity.

Confusion becomes clarity when you start listening to that still, small voice inside of you.

Find Your Cheerleaders

Everyone needs cheerleaders, whether we are getting unstuck or trying something brand-new. I value my cheerleaders so much, and I hope you have some in your corner too. But most of us also have to deal with haters. Some people who "knew you when" don't want you to forget where you came from. Ever. They will remind you of your shortcomings, bad decisions, and failures.

Please know this isn't a reflection of whether they love you. They probably do. But they don't want to see you living free because that convicts them of things they may not want to address in their own lives.

Your changing threatens the future of your relationship with them if they are stuck. They might worry that if you change, your relationship with them will change (and it probably will). They fear you will look at them differently (and you probably will). They fear you won't have time for them (and you may not). Those fears mean they will, often subconsciously, try to sink your ship before you can sail.

Of course, you and I both know that your trying something new has nothing to do with you thinking you're better than them. Wanting more for yourself does not mean you think less of them.

GET UNSTUCK & STAY UNSTUCK

We all grow and change over the course of our lifetimes, and not every friendship or relationship is made to last forever. It's absolutely okay to let go of people who are trying to sink your ship. You don't have to be angry with them or hate them. You can still love them and want what's best for them, but you don't have to let them keep putting you down and trying to keep you stuck. Pray for them. Love them. Then bless them and release them.

We need to establish and agree that it is okay for you to want more or different or better for your life, even if you aren't certain of what those things are. Wanting more does not mean you are unsatisfied with where you are. You can want more and still be content and grateful for what you already have.

We can adore our firstborn and still want another child.

We can love our body as it is and still aspire to change how we look in a swimsuit.

We can have a wonderful business and still want to take it to the next level.

We can be giving at church but still want to give more.

Wanting more does *not* necessarily come from a place of greed or jealousy or discontent. I think we were made to want more. God doesn't want us to settle for a so-so life on our own when we could have so much more with Him. He gives us more even when we don't think to ask for it. If God wants so much for us, I think we're allowed to want more for ourselves too.

Find the people in your life who are reaching for more for themselves. The women who refuse to stay stuck, even when it's hard. The moms who are listening to God's callings for them, even when those aren't things they had planned for themselves.

Look for the friends and family members who encourage you and cheer for you every step of the way. These are the folks who will mourn with you if things fall apart and celebrate with you when you succeed. They will never make you feel small or silly for trying something outside of your wheelhouse or for taking a big risk.

These are your people. Add them to your speed dial and fill your social calendar with plans with them. They are on fire to fulfill their purposes and will do everything they can to support you as you fulfill yours. These are the friends you deserve. Hold on to them tightly.

Make Prayer Your Priority

I've already talked a lot about this in this book, but it's so important that I'm going to repeat it again. You can do everything right but still end up stuck if you aren't living your life with God.

If you want to stay free, keep praying every day. Keep listening for God's wisdom and direction for your life. Keep paying attention to hear God's whispers and nudges. Keep saying, "Yes, Lord!" with all your heart when He calls you to something, whether it's big or small.

The way to get the life you're meant to live is not by doing whatever you want. If you've given God the highest place in your life, then you don't get to pick how God uses you. But you will be amazed by where He takes you. You cannot get stuck if you are doing what God tells you to do. Knowing that He is walking beside you will give you the strength you need, the wisdom to take the next step in His plan, and the confidence that you are doing what He wants because He is totally in it.

> Everything you want—a life of freedom and purpose and deep, abiding love—is on the other side of obedience to God.

Everything you want—a life of freedom and purpose and deep, abiding love—is on the other side of obedience to God.

So go ahead and say yes.

Let's pray.

Heavenly Father,

Thank You for preparing me for the way ahead. I know I'll hit resistance and have doubts and get distracted and possibly even get stuck again. Please help me to keep my feet on Your path, to keep moving forward with my eyes on You and Your plans for me in order to avoid sticky spots. Help me to find the people who will cheer me on and encourage me and who I can encourage too. I want the life of freedom You have planned for me and I'm listening for Your guidance. In Jesus' name, amen.

Friend, I am so incredibly excited for you. Pushing past your fear, confronting the behaviors and circumstances that have held you back, and finding ways to move forward into an unstuck life won't be easy, but it will be so worth it.

You have the chance to go from a life of struggle and stuck to something so much better. A life is waiting full of possibility, abundance, purpose, and all the good things God has planned for you. All you have to do is unstick. You've done the first part. You've read this book and answered the questions. Now you've got the inspiration, you've got the tools and plans, and (I hope!) you've got the motivation to make a change. Now it's time to go do the work. I'll be cheering you on all the way.

Heavenly Father,

I am so grateful for Your guidance and support in getting unstuck and staying that way. I'm saying yes, God. Yes to Your plans. Yes to Your timing. Yes to Your steps. Yes to anything You want for me. Bring it on. I want the life of freedom that only You can provide. I'm Yours. Let's do it. In Jesus' name, amen.

Jennifer Allwood has found freedom in her business, her time, her finances, and most importantly, her faith through years of releasing more and more over to God. What started as a desire to help pull her family out of financial desperation became a calling to help other women find the courage to do the same.

Jennifer stands steadfast in the idea of using her business to serve God and her family. Her goal is to use the tools so readily available—social media, email, the internet—as the way to make this happen. She knows getting unstuck, pushing through the overwhelm, and doing things despite fear are key in growing any business.

Today Jennifer uses her social media following of 500k people, including her podcast, *The Jennifer Allwood Show*, with over 3.5 million downloads; her coaching groups with thousands of members; and her #1 bestselling book, *Fear Is Not the Boss of You*, to help other women do for their businesses what she has done for her own.

Jennifer inspires women to believe that they are enough—she motivates them and gives them permission to lean into their calling. She's the best friend that will light a fire underneath them and cheer them on every step of the way.